D1040680

Sri Daya Mata

President and spiritual head of
Self-Realization Fellowship/Yogoda Satsanga Society of India

Intuition:
Soul-Guidance
—— *for* ——
Life's Decisions

Selections from the talks and writings of
Sri Daya Mata

Self-Realization Fellowship
FOUNDED 1920
Paramahansa Yogananda

ABOUT THIS BOOK: *Intuition: Soul-Guidance for Life's Decisions* is a compilation of selections from the talks and letters of Sri Daya Mata. The talks were given during informal gatherings in America and India at which she spoke on various aspects of the spiritual life. These have been published previously in *Self-Realization* magazine, and also in two anthologies, *Only Love* (1976), and *Finding the Joy Within You* (1990).

Authorized by the International Publications Council of
SELF-REALIZATION FELLOWSHIP
3880 San Rafael Avenue
Los Angeles, California 90065-3298

The Self-Realization Fellowship name and emblem (shown above) appear on all SRF books, recordings, and other publications, assuring the reader that a work originates with the society established by Paramahansa Yogananda and faithfully conveys his teachings.

Library of Congress Cataloging-in-Publication Data

Sri Daya Mata.
  Intuition : soul-guidance for life's decisions : selections from
  the talks and writings of Sri Daya Mata. — 1st ed.
    p. cm. — (How-to-live series)
  ISBN-13: 978-0-87612-465-9
  ISBN 0-87612-465-1
 1. Spiritual life. 2. Intuition. I. Title. II. Series.
BP605.S36 S75 2003
294.5'44 — dc21
              2003012237

Printed in the United States of America
1719-J1024

CONTENTS

PREFACE

"Self-realization is the knowing — in body, mind, and soul — that we are one with the omnipresence of God; that we do not have to pray that it come to us, that we are not merely near it at all times, but that God's omnipresence is our omnipresence; that we are just as much a part of Him now as we ever will be. All we have to do is improve our knowing."

— Paramahansa Yogananda

In his "how-to-live" teachings, Paramahansa Yogananda has given to people of all cultures, races, and creeds the means to free themselves from physical, mental, and spiritual inharmonies — to create for themselves a life of enduring happiness and all-round success.

The books in this series present Paramahansaji's how-to-live wisdom on many subjects — in his own words and in those of his close disciples — providing readers with spiritual insight and practical keys for bringing into daily life the inner balance and harmony that is the essence of yoga. Through the practice of meditation and the universal principles of right action and right attitude highlighted in these books, one can experience every moment as an opportunity to grow in awareness of the Divine.

While each book addresses a distinct topic, one message resonates throughout the series: *Seek God first.* Whether speaking of creating fulfilling relationships, raising spiritual children, overcoming self-defeating habits, or any of the other myriad goals and challenges of modern living, Paramahansa Yogananda again and again refocuses our attention towards life's highest attainment: Self-realization—knowing our true nature as divine beings. Through the inspiration and encouragement of his teachings, we learn how to live a truly victorious life—transcending limitations, fear, and suffering—by awakening to the infinite power and joy of our real Self: the soul.

— *Self-Realization Fellowship*

Intuition:
Soul-Guidance
for
Life's Decisions

Part I

INTRODUCTION

"Intuition is soul guidance, appearing naturally in man during those instants when his mind is calm. . . . The goal of yoga science is to calm the mind, that without distortion it may hear the infallible counsel of the Inner Voice."

— Paramahansa Yogananda,
in *Autobiography of a Yogi*

Every one of us can learn to move through life enjoying a radiant peace and serenity. Instead of permitting the inevitable complexities and demanding situations to make us nervous or emotionally upset, we should use each of them as motivation to open in ourselves a new window onto the Divine Consciousness. We can be constantly renewed by fresh inflows

3

of inspiration, understanding, and heavenly assurance if we resolve to maintain evenness of mind.

The *rishis* of India, said Paramahansa Yogananda, were the greatest psychological experts. And evenmindedness is their supreme prescription for psychological and emotional well-being: keeping the mind calm and unruffled, that we may behold and identify with the perfect soul-reflection of the Divine within us — ever blissful, never troubled.

Life is so often capricious, its course filled with unexpected twists and turns. Just when we feel content, successful, and at peace, some unforeseen circumstance takes us by surprise; or the buffeting of daily challenges erodes our good resolves. We are tossed again on the waves of duality, of health and sickness, joy and sorrow. There is only one way to maintain an unshakable inner tranquility. We cannot think ourselves into that state; we cannot achieve it through the beauties of nature or music or art or other outer experiences, no matter how peaceful they may make us feel. It comes only through deep, devotion-filled meditation that takes us beyond thought and emotion, anchoring us in the calm center of our being.

———— ◆ ————

Finding the Inner Certainty of Our Connection With the Divine

To walk inwardly with God is the state of the spiritual person. Each day, silence the body and still the mind, and turn your whole being within to commune with God. If you form that habit of meditation, it will make all the difference between your being an ordinary person, one who is uncertain, filled with doubts and frustrations, and a spiritual person, who feels that his life is completely in the hands of God and that therefore all is well with him.

Nothing in life or in death should make us fearful or upset. The marvelous guidance Paramahansa Yogananda gave us, for which I am forever grateful, instilled in us the awareness that life is eternal. For a short while the immortal ray of light that is our soul wears a perishable mortal garment — woman or man; black, white, red, or yellow — but for all eternity the soul is sustained by the Infinite Source of that light. The more we meditate, the more we feel that consciousness. And the less we meditate, the less able we are to transcend identification with the little self — so many pounds of flesh encasing a limited mind bound by sense perceptions to the troublesome environs of the world. We have to get to the Self beyond its physical and mental instrumentalities to realize we are not fragile mortal beings; there is an unbroken link between ourselves and the Beloved Mother of the universe, the Divine Consciousness flowing through us and permeating Infinity.

———•———

Guiding Our Daily Choice of Life's Many Options

The way to unite our consciousness with God-consciousness begins with our daily choice of thoughts and actions. Life places many options before us, often contradictory. We respond either to the pull of our senses, desires, and habits or to the still, small voice of conscience that reminds us wherein lies real happiness—using the divine strength of our discriminative will to make those choices that affirm by action God's consciousness and qualities within us.

———•———

Life tempts us with many diversions that seem to promise fulfillment; there is so much we want to do and to have. It is not wrong to pursue worthy ambitions—we were born to act and to exercise our initiative for doing good.

But how easy it is to become engrossed in our role, tying our happiness to the ever-changing ups and downs of our environment. We feel the pull of habits and of the wayward senses. Countless desires and demands of the ego clamor for attention....

It is up to us to choose whether the ego or the soul will guide the trend of our consciousness.*

* Ego: the delusory sense of identification with the body and limited human personality, which prevents awareness of one's true Self as soul—an individualized spark of the Divine Being.

Part II

DIFFICULT CHOICES, DAILY DECISIONS

Receiving Intuitive Direction From Your Soul

*Q*uestion: *Faced with the many difficult choices and conflicting options that are part of life in the day-to-day world, how can we discern whether a decision is the right one or whether it merely seems right because of our personal desires and an attachment to our own inclinations?*

First of all, we have to realize that for most people, the vast majority of their actions *are* tinged with personal desires. That is normal; it's human. In fact, it is the motivating power of their desires that makes accomplishment possible!

What the great ones teach is that we should

first concentrate on replacing harmful desires— those that keep us in mortal bondage—with wholesome ambitions that unfold our higher nature. In this way, as we are drawn closer to the Divine, we progress steadily toward true desirelessness—oneness with God, in which all desires have been eternally fulfilled. Until we reach that blessed state, our vision and judgment are influenced by desires—no question about it!

How to Choose Correctly
in Any Given Situation

To know how to choose correctly in any given situation, we need to guide our judgments by the power of intuition. We are all endowed with this "sixth sense," but most persons do not use it. Instead, they rely on the reports of five lower senses. But those five senses do not always supply the right data upon which we can react in the right way or make the right decisions. Aside from their limited scope and power, the senses (and their "master," the ego-identified mind) interpret things according to their own likes and dislikes rather than according to what is true and ultimately beneficial for the soul. Making decisions based only on what his external senses and lower mind tell him, it is no wonder man is so often in trouble!

I hope the day will come when the whole world will understand the importance of a daily period for going within for guidance and communion with God. By doing so, you become more balanced; you become calmer; your discriminative insight awakens. You become freer from those binding habits, desires, emotions, and attachments that impel you to behave in a certain way, right or wrong. Discrimination (which like intuition is a quality of the soul) enables you to discern the things you ought to do when you ought to do them. It is by meditation that these soul-faculties are developed.

Learn to Look at Situations Clearly, Without the "Blinders" of Emotion

When our discrimination is clouded by desires and emotions, it is a form of blindness — psychological and spiritual blindness. When people are under the sway of emotion, they become confused and are unable to reason clearly.

That was one of the points Paramahansa Yogananda often stressed to us....He would tell us, "Don't run around like a chicken with its head cut off!" In the early days he assigned so many responsibilities to me that it was difficult to keep calm, but I remember his saying to me: "You must become like steel inside. Don't get emotional."

Emotion prejudices you; it paralyzes your ability to think clearly and perceive a situation accurately....When we learn to separate facts from our opinions, then our judgment is not so much influenced by egoistic desires. If every human being would learn to do this, there would be much more understanding and peace in the world.

You see, these are practical points. Attaining and expressing Self-realization is what this path is all about: loving God, knowing our oneness with Him; and then bringing that love and realization down into practical application in our daily lives.

A Restless Mind Blocks Divine Guidance

So in learning to make right decisions, the first step I would suggest to you would be: Make meditation a regular part of your daily life. Without periods of interiorized meditation, your attention remains habitually concentrated externally in the sensory and mental impulses of nerves, producing nervous tension. In this constant state of restlessness, you cannot receive divine guidance from within.

The Bible says, "Be still, and know that I

am God."* Few in the West understand what
that really means: The more still you become,
the more you can tune in with the omnipresence of God. Yoga tells you how to achieve that
blessed stillness consciously. Paramahansa Yogananda gave us marvelous yoga techniques for
this purpose.†

Setting Aside the Ego's "Agenda"

Also, by meditation you become less bound
by your desires. It loosens those knots that tie
you to a personal agenda of likes and dislikes:
"This is what I want. I crave this; the 'right
course' is whatever will give it to me." You become more neutral, more objective. It is not
indifference or apathy; it is an expansion and

---

* Psalms 46:10.

† Taught in the *Self-Realization Fellowship Lessons* (see page 72).

"Yoga" refers not to physical postures and exercises (*Hatha
Yoga*), but to the classical system of psychophysical techniques
for awakening the higher Self and uniting it with the Divine.

clearing of the consciousness, vibrant with peace and happiness that flow from the presence of God in your soul.

Then when the question arises, "Is this the right thing to do?" you can stand back and impartially ask yourself, "Is this something I want, or is this something God wants for me?" When you have felt that peace in meditation, then say to God, "Lord, guide me." Keep on saying it— deeply, sincerely. Throughout the day, think of God: "Guide me, bless me." That keeps your mind receptive and open to inspiration, the silent guidance of God.

Intuitive Feelings Perceived in the Heart

"Intuition is perceived mostly through the heart," Paramahansaji said. This I have found. When something is not right, I get feelings here in the heart. There is an uneasiness that makes me think, "Oh, there is something wrong with that individual, or with that situation." It does not make me uncomfortable, but I am conscious of a little disturbance in my heart. This is what Paramahansaji is referring to. "Whenever you are concerned about something, or trying to find the right course to pursue, calmly concentrate on the heart. Don't try to analyze the problem; just remain watching the heart."

Of course, it is good to sit quietly and think deeply about your problem after meditation; that has its place as well. But as you go about your duties, when the thought of your problem arises, just put your mind at the heart center. Concentrate there, and try to be aware of the feelings that are flowing from that center.

Paramahansaji goes on to say: "Remain calm, and then suddenly a great feeling will come over you and your intuition will point you to the right step you should take at that time. If your mind and emotions are calm and attuned to the voice of intuition within, you will be rightly guided. In your everyday life, you will meet the right people who will bring some solution to your problem, or who will help you in some way — or through their contact and counsel, you will find the right way."

This is a great truth, and I urge all of you to put it into practice. If you persist, you will learn to recognize and be led by the "still small voice" within.

Remain Flexible and Receptive to New Directions

However, it doesn't happen overnight; do not think as a beginner that you can abandon reason and common sense "because my intuition is guiding me." Through your persistent prayers for guidance and your calm receptivity, an inner sense will prompt you as to the best way to proceed. When that happens, go forward with full faith; but all the while remain flexible: "It seems to me that this is the right way to go.

But if at any time, Lord, You show me that I have made the wrong choice, I can step back; I can accept correction."

Sometimes we get so infatuated with our own ideas or wonted way of doing things that we strongly resent any suggestion that some other way might be better or equally acceptable. Perhaps at work you have gone to a lot of effort to prepare a proposal, but your ideas are rejected. The ego-bound individual will get upset over such treatment. But that isn't the right attitude. Do not be the type of person who is irrationally attached to his own idea—it's his "baby" and you had better use it or else! This is emotional blindness; stubbornly clinging to an idea just because it is "ours" prevents us from recognizing opportunities to expand our perception and understanding.

I remember several times when Paramahansaji gave the same project to two or three different disciples to work on independently. I used to wonder why he was doing that, because obviously he intended to use the finished product of only one of them. But gradually I came to see his twofold purpose: He was getting them to think, to use their minds in a creative way in developing projects; and he was training them to be nonattached to what they do.

Whatever you do, do it with enthusiasm, with a sense of joy—but think of it this way: "I did it for You, my God. I give the fruits of this labor to You." In the midst of your work, at the beginning of your work, and at the close of your work, make a mental surrender of your efforts, an offering of your actions at the feet of God. This is the way to overcome the ego, and to develop receptivity to God's guidance and will. Without that, we are continually led astray by subtle but persuasive egoistic compulsions, which appear "wise" because they agree with our deep-seated tendencies and desires.

Purity of Heart and Mind
Make One Receptive

Jesus said, "Lord...Thou hast hid these things from the wise and prudent, and hast revealed them unto babes."* These words refer to the purity of the child's nature: trusting, pure, loving—not having yet taken on the habits that result from dealing with this world. It is said that up until the age of seven or eight, the child's consciousness is not fully immersed in this world. That is why not infrequently one hears children say wondrous things and refer to the life beyond this life, because they have just come from that astral realm. Unless they have been very materialistic in previous lives, their minds and hearts are still pure until the world catches them again.

"Wise and prudent," on the other hand, does not always mean pure. A person may be so

---

* Matthew 11:25.

enamored of his own intellect that he becomes self-satisfied; he thinks he knows best about everything. To that kind, God does not reveal Himself. He responds to those who have the simple, loving, trustful nature of a child toward the mother—open and receptive. This relationship with God can be cultivated by keeping the consciousness more aloof from the influence of desires and emotions and attachments.

Keep the Mind at the Center of Spiritual Awareness

The average individual's consciousness dwells primarily on the sensory surface of the body, which is enlivened by the lower *chakras* of the spine.* That is why he is always in a state of

---

* Yoga teaches that within man's brain and spinal plexuses are seven subtle centers of life and consciousness. Without the specialized powers lodged therein, the body would be an inert mass of clay. Man's materialistic instincts and motivations have their correlative powers in the externalization of the energies in

21

restlessness and worldly consciousness. In the ashram we are taught to keep our minds always at the Christ center — always. One of the first things Paramahansa Yogananda taught me when I came to him was, "Let the mind always rest here at this center (the point between the eyebrows)." Herein is the polestar of spiritual consciousness, the center where we commune with God. The more the attention is focused there, the more power we draw from the higher centers of spiritual perception in the spine — from the heart center and above.

Throughout the day, the clock pendulum swings back and forth, keeping track of the changing hours. It is doing its duty, isn't it? But when that pendulum stops, where does it rest?

---

the lower three subtle spinal *chakras*. The higher centers are the fountainhead of divine feeling and inspiration and spiritual perception. According to the nature of man's thoughts and desires, his consciousness is drawn to and concentrated in the corresponding center of power and activity.

Not out here, or over there, but right in the center. So should it be with us: We all have our duties in this world, but whenever there is a gap in between activities, our attention should be centered here at the *Kutastha,* the seat of Christ Consciousness.*

Question: *How do we learn to keep the attention at the* Kutastha *even during the activity of the day?*

Only one way: through practice. When you

---

* The Christ or *Kutastha* center is the center of concentration and will in the body, at the point between the eyebrows (*ajna chakra*)—the seat of Christ Consciousness (*Kutastha Chaitanya*) and of the spiritual eye. "Christ" or "Christ Consciousness" is the projected consciousness of God immanent in all creation. In Christian scripture it is called the "only begotten son," the only pure reflection in creation of God the Father; in Hindu scripture it is called *Kutastha Chaitanya,* the cosmic intelligence of Spirit everywhere present in creation. It is the universal consciousness, oneness with God, manifested by Jesus, Krishna, and other avatars. Great saints and yogis know it as the state of *samadhi* meditation wherein their consciousness has become identified with the intelligence in every particle of creation; they feel the entire universe as their own body.

are carrying on your duties, your attention should be on what you are doing; that is vital. But every now and then throughout the day it is possible to stop for a moment — whatever you are doing, anywhere — and just let the mind rest at the *Kutastha.*

Truthfully, it becomes automatic after a while. When I'm busy with many things in connection with Paramahansaji's work, every now and then I'll pause and turn my mind within; in an instant that throbbing presence of the Divine is there — that joyous, loving presence of God. This you will find, if you cultivate the habit. Anytime you have a few moments free, sit quietly, bring the mind back to the *Kutastha,* and say, "My Lord, bless me" — or some other simple thought that comes from your heart.

As time goes on, you will find that more and more your mind rests at that point, no matter what you are doing. Your consciousness becomes spiritualized.

Wisdom and Inner Strength to Be Victorious in Life

These are the qualities that endow us with the ability to choose correctly when life's decisions are before us:

- Inner calmness, the condition in which our intuitive and discriminative faculties can awaken;
- an effort to be less emotional and more objective, stepping back from our personal attachments and prejudices;
- a humble turning to God for guidance rather than to our own "wisdom."

The development of all these qualities begins with, and is nurtured by, daily deep meditation.

How nice it would be if God were to say, "Now, My child, you just sit back and I'll tell you exactly what to do and when to do it. You follow this and your life will be a bed of roses!" But it isn't that way. If He did that, we would

25

not develop our own divine nature. We couldn't; for it is by struggle and by exercising our God-given discrimination that our divinity is revealed. We must bring it out of ourselves.

Until we do, we will never truly realize that we are a part of Him. Intellectually we may understand it, but that is of little practical value. Only when we have direct realization of truth — when we have faced all life's trials and found within ourselves the divine guidance and strength to be victorious — can we say with conviction, as did Christ and all the great ones: "I and my Father are one; I *know* it. I am made in His indomitable image."

Thus will we play our part in the Lord's *lila*, the divine drama of life, with the courage and faith and wisdom of a child of God.

Part III

SOLVING YOUR PROBLEMS
WITH GUIDANCE
FROM WITHIN

Paramahansa Yogananda often quoted this saying: "The Lord helps him who helps himself." When having to make a decision, we would like nothing better than for some divine force to just tell us what to do. It would be so easy; we would not have to make any effort if at any given moment we knew we were receiving God's direct guidance.

But it is not meant to be so simple, and the reason is this: We are a part of God, but we don't know it—and we will never know it if all we do is put the burden on Him and say, "You tell me what to do," as though we were dumb puppets and He the Puppeteer. No, He expects us to use the mind He has given to us, *while* asking His guidance.

The Ultimate Prayer

Jesus prayed the ultimate prayer: "Lord, let Thy will be done." Now, many people interpret this to mean that they are not supposed to do any willing or thinking at all, but just sit and meditate, and wait for God to do something through them. This is wrong. We are made in His image. He gave man intelligence such as He gave to no other creature, and He expects us to use it. This is why Paramahansaji taught us to pray:

> *"Lord, I will reason, I will will, I will act;*
> *but guide Thou my reason, will, and activity*
> *to the right thing that I should do."*

We practice this religiously in the ashram. In our meetings about the work, we meditate for a few minutes and then offer that prayer. Only then do we enter into discussion and make decisions.

So do not sit back and expect God to initiate the necessary actions. Applying the principles of reason, will, and action, pursue what seems to be the best course. Work conscientiously, using your will and intelligence, and at the same time pray throughout: "Lord, guide me; let me follow Thy will. Only Thy will be done."

By doing this, you keep your mind receptive to His guidance. You may then find that you will suddenly see clearly, "No, I must go in this direction now." God shows you the way. But remember, when asking God to guide you, your mind must never be closed; let it be always open and receptive. This is how God helps him who helps himself. It works, but the initiative and effort have to come from us.

You do not have to live in an ashram in order to serve God and follow His will. Each one of us is at this moment where God and our past actions have placed us. If you are not satisfied with your present condition, meditate and ask God's guidance. But while doing so, apply your God-given reason. Analyze the options you have in connection with your life and your future.

Conscience and Intuition: *the Divine Voice Within*

The Divine Voice within us will help us to solve all our problems. The voice of the conscience is a God-given instrument of divine guidance in every human being. But in many, it is not heard because over a period of one or countless lives they have refused to pay any attention to it. Consequently, that voice becomes silent, or very, very faint. But as an individual begins to put right behavior into action in his life, the inner whispers grow stronger again.

Beyond the semi-intuitive conscience is pure intuition, the soul's direct perception of truth —the infallible Divine Voice.

All of us are endowed with intuition. We have the five physical senses, and also a sixth sense—all-knowing intuition. We relate to this world through the five physical senses: we touch, hear, smell, taste, and see. In most people, the sixth sense, intuitive feeling, remains undeveloped from lack of use. Blindfold the eyes from childhood, and years later when that blindfold is removed, everything will appear flat. Or immobilize the arm, and it will not develop properly for lack of use. Similarly, through lack of use, intuition no longer functions in many.

Meditation Develops the Power of Intuition

But there is a way to develop intuition. The sixth sense is not able to function until we quiet the body and the mind. So the first step in developing intuition is meditation, entering a state of inner calmness. The more deeply you meditate, and then put your mind on some problem, the more your intuitive power will express itself in resolving that problem. That power develops gradually, not all at once; just as a muscle or limb is strengthened gradually by exercise — it doesn't happen overnight....

Intuition can be developed by those persons who are deeply contemplative, those who have reached by meditation that state of absolute calmness of heart and mind. One must be neither overcome by emotion nor bound by intellect. Intuition is a blend of thinking (the thought process) and the heart (the feeling process). Many people have intuitive experience through reason — a sort of guidance of their thoughts. In my own case, very often intuition expresses itself through feeling. When I have certain feelings about things or persons, those impressions are like subtle vibrations around my heart, and then I know, from years of experience, that these intimations are correct.

When you have developed intuition to some

degree, you will find that as you make decisions, something within you says: "This is the right way to go." That is intuition guiding you. Do not expect this to happen all at once. There will be some mistakes in the beginning as other factors within you impede the flow of intuition. But as you go on practicing meditation, and living more in the state of interior calmness bestowed by this practice, you will find increasing improvement in the development of your intuitive power.

Very often now, when something comes before my mind, I see not just the present matter, but projecting ahead, I see the end result. That is intuition. And if you act on it, you will find that everything runs smoothly — well, not always. Even though you have made the right decision, there will be some rough times. They are part of the growing process, learning how to deal with conditions that are normal in life. But your intuition tells you that even though there are problems, you have taken the right course of action.

Distinguishing Intuitive Guidance From Imagination

Learn to distinguish when inner "guidance" is an authentic intuitive message, or only imagination or emotionalism (which in some people are very strong, and are sometimes misinterpreted as intuition). You can recognize intuition if whatever guidance you feel from your experience produces the correspondingly right result. If the effects are contrary, you know it was nothing but imagination. Intuition will always bring forth the correct positive response for the good of one's own life or that of someone else. Only time and experience will enable you to tell always whether a strong inclination is imagination or a natural, intuitive feeling.

Part IV

THE VALUE OF SCIENTIFIC
TECHNIQUES OF MEDITATION

More and more people nowadays are realizing the tremendous benefits of meditation. They may read books on this subject or listen to spiritual teachers who advise, "Practice silence; go within." But multitudes who try it find themselves asking, "What on earth does that mean?"

Even though you may be sitting quietly, if your mind is filled with restless thoughts you are not truly silent. In the beginning when you sit to meditate, the mind is on a million things —you are thinking of all the work you should be doing; of the problems that have been upsetting you; of what you are going to do once you finish meditating.

Merely to tell someone to "practice silence" does not give him the means to quiet the thoughts. But when he is given a definite technique of controlling the mind to practice, he begins to understand that meditation means much more than merely shutting out the sights and sounds of the outer world; it is stilling the body and mind to such a degree that the consciousness becomes like a calm, crystal-clear lake, able to reflect the blissful presence of God.

Learning to Quiet and Interiorize the Mind

To achieve this, one must take the scattered attention and with great determination, patience, and calmness center it upon one thing. A diffused light has no power. But when a magnifying glass is placed under sunlight, it can be positioned in such a way that the sun's rays become focused — intense enough to ignite a piece of paper that is placed beneath the glass.

This is what happens when one practices the *Hong-Sau* Technique of Concentration. The mind becomes like a precise instrument, so perfectly focused that one's attention remains one-pointedly upon God. When you have practiced faithfully for many years, you find that in an instant you can attune yourself with God. That is the power of this technique.

There are various methods of meditation. However, one standard principle is applicable to everyone, regardless of what path or religion they follow: Unless and until you practice a technique that develops the powers of concentration and interiorizes the mind, you will never know God. The methods we teach in Self-Realization Fellowship — the techniques of *Hong-Sau,* meditation on *Aum,* and *Kriya Yoga* — are the ones that our guru, Paramahansaji, after searching throughout India, found to be most efficacious for achieving *pratyahara* — complete mental interiorization — and the higher states

of Self-realization.* If you practice these techniques faithfully, you will attain that goal, without fail. If you are not progressing, it means
only that you are not practicing them regularly,
deeply, and correctly according to the rules you
have been given.

The Scientific Steps to Successful Meditation

There are definite scientific principles that
must be applied in the search for God. These
are the principles of yoga, which in India have
been researched, practiced, and proven for cen-
turies....The science of religion is based on
laws that never change.

---

* The science of yoga, as expounded by the sage Patanjali—the
foremost ancient exponent of yoga—is based upon eight steps by
which man attains union with God: (1) *yama*, moral conduct; (2)
niyama, religious observances; (3) *asana*, right posture to still bodily
restlessness; (4) *pranayama*, control of *prana*, subtle life currents; (5)
pratyahara, interiorization; (6) *dharana*, concentration; (7) *dhyana*,
meditation; and (8) *samadhi*, the ecstasy of oneness with God.

I have had people ask, "Why should my relationship with God be governed by so many rules? Can't I simply be guided by my own intuitive feelings on the spiritual path?" In answer I say, "By all means be guided by your intuition, but first be sure that it really *is* intuition, which comes from attunement with God, and not just your subconscious desire to do what you want to do."

Erroneous self-determination is a pitfall for many people. First follow the science; learn to realize God through proper application of the methods of yoga. When you know Him beyond any doubt — when you can be so even-minded that through all of life's experiences you retain an attitude of blissful devotion to God, of constant self-surrender at His feet — then there is the possibility of your spiritual endeavors being guided by intuition, not before.

The great masters have shown us the steps that they themselves took to reach God-realization. Anyone who has common sense will follow them, rather than try to forge their own way. Why would you want to "reinvent the wheel"? You have freedom to do so, of course; but is it not more logical to take the path that has already been proved to lead to God, rather than spending years, perhaps incarnations, trying to find your own way through laborious trial-and-error experimentation?

The laws are known; depth in meditation comes from their patient, steadfast application. It is like learning to play the piano. Success is unlikely through unscientific "hit-and-miss" attempts. Before you can play a Rachmaninoff piano concerto, you need to know where the right keys are, and then gradually become skilled by diligent daily practice. It is the same with meditation. It requires application of the scientific steps of *yama, niyama, asana,* and a continuous determination to persevere in your practice of *pranayama* techniques until the thoughts become completely still. Through

Hong-Sau your mind and breath become perfectly synchronized; it is as if they become forged into one razor-sharp sword that suddenly severs the inner fetters that were binding you. The mind becomes free and clear. You feel within yourself the presence of God just behind this physical form, behind all life. Such marvelously thrilling perceptions come when you practice the science of meditation.

Part V

PRACTICAL GUIDANCE FOR MAKING INTUITIVE DECISIONS

*Q**uestion:** "If we have to make an immediate decision and we seem unable to have the inner contact with God that will give us guidance, how should we act?"*

First I would ask you, what do you mean by "contact with God"? Are you expecting Him to appear to you in a vision and give you precise instructions about what to do? That is not how we grow spiritually.

Instead of expecting miraculous demonstrations, the real devotee strives for inward attunement of his mind and feelings with the Divine.

Those who meditate know what that state of attunement feels like: The moment you take your mind within, you feel that peace, that awareness of the presence of God. He is always there; He is never away. We discover this through meditation; and we can hold on to that awareness during activity by practicing the Presence, by trying always to live in the conscious thought of God.

If circumstances permit, before making an important determination sit quietly for a few moments and deeply pray for guidance to make the right choice. Do not let it be absentminded mental wandering; talk to God or Guru—and mean it. After meditating and praying about your decision, put your consciousness on the feeling in your heart. Ask yourself, and try to feel, which course appeals to your heart and to your common sense. And then act—make your decision then and there.

Do Not Be Timid

Do not be afraid to make decisions. Some people are so timid about deciding that they never act with resolve and determination. Indecisiveness is a great blight on the character. It is really much better to make some decision than to take no action at all; because even if you decide wrongly, you will learn by it and will have gained mental strength by trying. If you remain passive, the only thing you will learn is that you are a powerless victim of circumstances. Instead, have the courage to face your challenges with decisiveness.

When the responsibility for Paramahansa Yogananda's work was placed on my shoulders,*

---

* In the late 1940s Sri Daya Mata was appointed by Paramahansa Yogananda to be in charge of the International Headquarters of his worldwide society. In 1955, three years after the Guru's passing, she became president and spiritual head of Self-Realization Fellowship/Yogoda Satsanga Society of India. (*Publisher's Note*)

I was overly anxious lest I make a mistake! Then I heard something that was very helpful: accomplished businesspeople consider themselves successful if they are right sixty percent of the time. In other words, they allow themselves forty percent error. So I told myself, "Surely I can do at least that well!"

There is no need to be overly worried if you make a mistake. Do not punish yourself; instead, recognize you have erred and correct it. Learn from it, and go on. Always remember: The moment you begin a sincere search for God, you can know for certain that He is not going to fail you. Lift up one hand toward Him, and He will stretch out both His hands to you. I know this to be so; it cannot be otherwise. This faith will grow in you as you progress on the spiritual path.

So, when faced with a decision, what you should do is simply this: Pray, try to feel an inner attunement. If you don't feel it, meditate for a few moments, or for as much time as you have available. From that center of calmness, then make your decision. Do not sit and wait for some tremendous message to come to you written in lightning!

These are the practical, down-to-earth truths that are the basis of the spiritual life. The Divine is very practical — He is in His heaven, but He is also right here on earth with you. That is the way we all should be — our consciousness in God, our actions tending to our God-given duties.

———•◆•———

Spiritual Maturity: Facing Problems With Calmness and Strength

To be receptive in this way one must be relaxed mentally. Paramahansa Yogananda used to say that sometimes people try so hard to understand that their minds race off in all directions and consequently they don't understand anything. He would sometimes remind us, "You're trying too hard!"

We used to think of all the things we needed to ask Paramahansaji, but when we were with him, and he turned our minds toward God, those questions did not seem important at all.

Very often our so-called problems are the result of immature thinking. In our Guru's presence, our minds became calm and the inner tension and restlessness created by our problems and questions were completely erased. Although there may have been no discussion, when we returned to our duties, our thoughts formed more clearly, and we felt the assurance of an inner sense of direction.

He didn't do our thinking for us. He taught us to "grow up," because maturity and spiritual growth go hand in hand. We cannot make any real progress if we remain dependent on others. Maturity means the ability to face life's problems with strength and objective calmness, and to be able to concentrate with discriminative intelligence on finding the best solution. Spiritual maturity comes by drawing closer to God, so that intuitive perception and understanding deepen.

Guidance and Strength Through Faith in God

In the latter years of his life, Paramahansaji spent much time in the desert, working on his writings. He left me in charge at Mt. Washington. I had to face an endless avalanche of organizational problems. I could rarely talk to my Guru about them because he was no longer in the consciousness of the day-to-day travails of a worldwide society. He was more withdrawn, in continual divine communion in *samadhi*. What was I to do? I could sit in my room and bemoan my situation, or I could tell him I simply could not carry the responsibility. I considered all alternatives, but no avenue of escape would bring me inner peace.

In the final analysis, I knew there was no other recourse than to surrender. Mentally, I said to myself: "I will just do my best each day. I may make mistakes, but God knows I will be trying my utmost to follow His will. There is only one way to free myself from the tremendous pressure imposed by this responsibility: I will place my faith, without any reservation, in God." What a great lesson that experience taught me.

After that, whenever a feeling of being burdened came over me, I would mentally throw myself at the feet of God, knowing that He alone could give me the strength and guidance necessary to carry on.

That test went on, in greater or lesser degree, for some years. But by enduring and persevering with a positive attitude, one day I could say, "Now I see what it means to have total faith in God." Such faith has to come not only from the head, but also from the heart;

and for faith to become strong, one has to keep on practicing it every day of his life.

Part VI

SURRENDER: CONNECTING WITH THE UNLIMITED POWER OF GOD

At one time or another every one of us reaches a point at which our problems seem so overwhelming that we feel we cannot cope with them. We say to ourselves, "I've reached the end of my rope—physically, mentally, and emotionally. I've tried everything I can think of. What on earth can I do now?" Many people seek the help of a medical doctor or a psychiatrist; this is sound common sense. But there comes a time when the doctors can do nothing for us. What then?

I very much believe in the power of surrender to God, of placing our lives totally in His hands. He can bring us through every crisis, regardless of the dire pronouncements of any human being. I have been through many illnesses and have never let go of that Divine Power, because I know It sustains me. Time and again He has given me proof of this.

To draw on God's unlimited power, we need to develop more trust and faith in Him. Paramahansa Yogananda once said to me, "Inwardly hold always to the thought: 'Lord, let Thy will be done, not mine.'" Too often, people are afraid to surrender to God because they do not really trust Him. They are not sure if what He will give to them will be what they want. So even if they say, "Thy will be done," they do not mean it sincerely. That is where they make their mistake.

So long as we think we can run our lives by ourselves, we do not make contact with God. The delusion that the little ego is sufficient has to be abandoned before we can receive from the Divine. How many become lost because of the notion, "I can do it by myself." No, we can't! We cannot even breathe, we cannot even lift one little finger by ourselves. Every moment we are totally dependent on the Divine; every instant He sustains us....

Removing the Blocks to Deeper Levels of Consciousness

The mind as an instrument for tapping the power of God is limitless; I want to emphasize this to you all, as Paramahansaji did to those of us around him....Years ago he told us (and psychologists nowadays would certainly agree) that chronic worry, fear, nervous tension, and the other negative emotions—guilt, hate, jealousy, bitterness—close off the channels through which wisdom and healing flow from the deeper levels of consciousness. People become so tense and anxiety-ridden in struggling with their problems that they get emotionally "hung up."

So when we have tried everything possible

to solve our problem and nothing seems to do any good, the wisest course is simply this: *Relax.* Stop trying to deal with it through the limited human resources of the rational mind, which has brought you to your present state of frustration and tension. Surrender the problem to the Divine with one hundred percent faith and trust. In other words, "Let go and let God."

Is that not what the scriptures of every religion have taught? Endeavor to surrender fully to God your heart, your mind, your life. This will begin to remove the mental blocks that give you the consciousness of separation from Him. Accordingly, you will find His power flowing into you in a greater way. Creative thinkers, inventors, people who perform extraordinary feats of strength in moments of emergency, saints who commune with God—all successful human beings—have learned in varying degrees to tap that divine reservoir within, the sole source of creative inspiration and power.

Psychiatrists would say that these qualities reside in the "unconscious" mind.* They may not use the word God, because science looks at everything in terms of natural laws. But you cannot separate God from His laws. Regardless of what terminology is used, everyone who looks deeply enough will discover the similarity between the scientific principles governing the universe — including man's body and mind — and those truths spoken of by God-knowing seers throughout the ages. Any science that denies the existence of these spiritual truths has not yet fully understood that which it is studying. There is, in fact, no conflict between the spiritual teacher who says, "Have faith in God," and the psychiatrist who says, "Draw on the

* Paramahansa Yogananda referred to the subconscious and superconscious minds rather than the "unconscious." He said: "There is no actual *unconsciousness*; consciousness may sleep or rest, but it can never be unconscious. In sleep the consciousness is resting, i.e., not active. The soul is never unconscious."

55

inner resources of the unconscious mind." It is by contacting the deeper levels of the mind that we begin to perceive God.*

The tendency in our time, especially in the West, has been to try to divorce the universe and its beings from God. Nowadays, however, we see that many people are trying to get out of the ruts of materialistic thinking; they are seeking again the deeper metaphysical experiences of the mystics of old. Unfortunately, they often errone-ously assume that by getting out of the mislead-ing old ruts they are not going to fall into any new ones. But they do. For instance, some have tried to explore the inner realms through drugs, which only confuse the mind and distort the un-derstanding of what is real and what is unreal. Some people become fascinated by hypnosis, trance channeling, or other methods of passively attaining altered states of consciousness. All of

* "The kingdom of God is within you" (Luke 17:21).

these have dangerous pitfalls; all of them lead their practitioners to get into a whole new set of mental ruts. The only way to keep from getting "hung up" in this world is to become anchored in God. Then you are not hung up; you are soundly anchored!

The mind is a wonderful world whose powers should be investigated, but through the proper methods. The real spiritual seeker follows the right way—meditation taught by one who knows God—and he never loses touch with reality or common sense or the eternal laws of truth.

Relaxation and Meditation: Keys to Tapping Inner Resources of Strength

Whether one defines it as "tapping the power of the unconscious mind" or as "making contact with God," meditation is the highest way of finding the strength to overcome life's obstacles. Everyone should arrange his schedule in order to have time daily to free the mind from worries, responsibilities, and outer disturbances, so that he can give himself up to the thought of God in meditation....

- Sit up straight—spine erect—in a chair or cross-legged on a cushion.
- Close your eyes to reduce distractions; gently lift your gaze to the Christ center.*
- Tense and relax your body a few times while inhaling and exhaling deeply; and then let go, mentally and physically. Maintain the erect posture, but consciously relax all undue tension in the muscles. Make yourself as limp as a wet noodle hanging on the rigid rod of the spine.

---

* Paramahansa Yogananda explained that the position of one's eyes has a definite correlation to one's state of consciousness: lowered or downcast eyes correspond with subconsciousness (and tend to produce that state); eyes focused straight ahead are indicative of the conscious, active state of outer consciousness; and eyes uplifted help to elevate the mind to superconciousness.

Do not think about your problem; otherwise you will remain stuck on the conscious level. Practice *Kriya* and the other techniques, and deeply surrender heart, mind, and life to the Divine. When we relax and calm the mind by meditation, we begin to draw on the higher levels of consciousness, the eternal vault in which resides everything we have learned in this life and in our countless previous incarnations. When we tap the superconsciousness—the intuitive, all-knowing insight of the soul—wisdom begins to percolate up into the awareness, and we find a solution to our difficulty or guidance in the right direction....

The Value of Challenges and Struggles

When I look back over my own life and remember my early years on the spiritual path, I am grateful for every hard struggle that I have had to go through. These have brought out of me strength and determination and a total surrender to God and His will that I might not have developed in any other way.

Often, when we get sick or experience some crisis in our lives, we feel helpless and want to give up. But don't you know that facing and overcoming problems is what life is all about? That is why we are here — not to whine or despair, but to accept what comes to us and use it as a means to bring us into a closer relationship with God. When adversity strikes, do not think it is because God has forsaken you. Nonsense! If in those moments of trial you turn to Him in childlike trust, you will find Him with you, perhaps even more tangibly than He ever was during the good times in life.

The Power of Positive Attitude and Affirmation

No matter what happens, constantly look to the bright side: "Never mind, soon things will be better." By God's grace that is something I always have: hope. I never allow myself to become depressed. But I had to work at developing this, and all of you should do the same. Some people have a tendency to look always to the dark side of a situation. Invariably, their reaction to suggestions or conditions is one of negation or fear or pessimism. Scan your conduct every day, and if you catch yourself thinking or behaving in this way, remind yourself that this is the wrong attitude; it destroys peace, happiness, and constructive will. Yes, there is evil in this world; in the realm of duality there cannot be light without dark, joy without sorrow, health without sickness, life without death. But to dwell constantly on the negative side is an insult to the soul and to God. Never give in to discouragement!

Create an atmosphere of positive thinking around yourself. It has been said that to the mind, attitudes are more important than facts; and this is very true. If we consciously look for the best in every situation, that positive spirit and enthusiasm acts as a wonderful stimulant to the mind and feelings, and to the body. Right attitude is a tremendous help in removing the mental and emotional obstructions that cut us off from the divine resources within us.

Paramahansa Yogananda gave us a perfect example of positive thinking. He went through untold struggles in building this work of Self-Realization Fellowship and Yogoda Satsanga Society in India, but we never saw him dejected or complaining. And he would not permit us to be discouraged, either. He taught us to pray, "Divine Mother, teach me to stand unshaken midst the crash of breaking worlds." In other words, "No matter what happens in my life, I will never admit defeat, because You are with me. It is You who have given me life, and it is You who sustain me."

Develop this kind of adamant will power. In the midst of all crises, affirm with deep conviction, "Lord, I *can* succeed, for You are in me." Then set your will on trying to find a solution. You will see that in mysterious ways the Divine Power is helping you. While making your best effort, keep your mind in attunement with the inner Source of strength and guidance by affirming, "Lord, Thy will be done, not mine." That is the secret.

Affirmation, as Paramahansaji taught us, is an excellent way of tapping the power of the mind.* When you are troubled or fearful, for example, affirm with each breath, "Thou art in me; I am in Thee." You will feel the assurance of His presence.

In India this science of continuous repetition of a spiritual thought is known as *Japa Yoga;* in the West it is called practicing the presence of God. Affirmations repeated over and over

---

* See *Scientific Healing Affirmations,* by Paramahansa Yogananda, published by Self-Realization Fellowship.

with concentration and will power sink into the subconscious and superconscious minds, which respond by creating the very conditions we are affirming.

Spiritual Growth Comes by Daily Effort to Change Ourselves

That is how we change. We do not have to remain as we are; we needn't become "psychological furniture," as Paramahansaji used to say. Furniture never changes. If it were in its original form, a living tree, it would go on growing and producing; but when it is molded into a chair or a table it stops improving. It just gets older and deteriorates and falls apart.

To grow spiritually we must be trying constantly to change ourselves. Spirituality is not something that can be grafted onto us from without—a "halo" we can fashion and put on our heads. It comes from a continual, day-by-day, patient endeavor and a relaxed sense of surrender to the Divine. It isn't that suddenly the light of God descends on us and makes us instant saints. No; it is a daily effort to change ourselves and to surrender heart, mind, and soul to God, in meditation and in activity....

Wherever God has placed you, do the best you can to manifest a positive spirit, an inner strength of mind, a sense of faith and trust and surrender at His feet. It is so simple to know God; just let go and let Him enter your life. This is the whole purpose of the spiritual path. Accept each experience that comes to you as coming from Him, and try to learn from it. ...Do not remain the same old "psychological antique"; use God's power within you to change your life. Therein lies complete freedom from all limitations of body, mind, and this world of delusion. Therein lies the supreme victory for all of us.

Make the Lord the Shepherd of your soul. Make Him your Searchlight when you move along a shadowy pathway in life. He is your Moon in the night of ignorance. He is your Sun during the wakeful hours. And He is your Polestar on the dark seas of mortal existence. Seek His guidance.

The world will go on like this in its ups and downs. Where shall we look for a sense of direction? Not to the prejudices roused within us by our habits and the environmental influences of our families, our country, or the world; but to the guiding voice of Truth within.

—Paramahansa Yogananda,
in *The Divine Romance*

About the Author

Sri Daya Mata, whose name means "Mother of Compassion," has inspired people of all faiths and from all walks of life with her wisdom and great love of God, cultivated through her own practice of daily meditation and prayer for more than 70 years. The foremost living disciple of Paramahansa Yogananda, she entered the monastic order he established at the age of 17. In 1955 she became one of the first women in modern history to be appointed head of a worldwide religious movement. As president of Self-Realization Fellowship, the spiritual and humanitarian society Paramahansa Yogananda founded in 1920, Daya Mata has made several global speaking tours, and two anthologies of her lectures and informal talks have been published: *Only Love: Living the Spiritual Life in a Changing World* and *Finding the Joy Within You: Personal Counsel for God-Centered Living.*

Other Books and Recordings by Sri Daya Mata

Books

Only Love: Living the Spiritual Life in a Changing World

Finding the Joy Within You:
  Personal Counsel for God-Centered Living

Enter the Quiet Heart:
  Creating a Loving Relationship With God

CDs

Karma Yoga: Balancing Activity and Meditation

Moral Courage: Effecting Positive Change Through
  Moral and Spiritual Choices

The Way to Peace, Humility, and Love for God

Free Yourself From Tension

Audiocassettes

God First

Understanding the Soul's Need for God

Let Us Be Thankful

Anchoring Your Life in God

Is Meditation on God Compatible With Modern Life?

Living a God-Centered Life

Let Every Day Be Christmas

DVDs/Videocassettes

Him I Shall Follow: Remembrances of My Life With
  Paramahansa Yogananda

A Scripture of Love

Living in the Love of God

Security in a World of Change

The Second Coming of Christ: Making of a Scripture—
Reminiscences by Sri Daya Mata and Sri Mrinalini
Mata (DVD Only)

About Paramahansa Yogananda

Paramahansa Yogananda (1893–1952) is widely regarded as one of the preeminent spiritual figures of our time. Born in northern India, he came to the United States in 1920, where he taught India's ancient science of meditation and the art of balanced spiritual living for more than thirty years. Through his acclaimed life story, *Autobiography of a Yogi,* and his numerous other books, Paramahansa Yogananda has introduced millions of readers to the perennial wisdom of the East. Today his spiritual and humanitarian work is carried on by Self-Realization Fellowship, the international society he founded in 1920 to disseminate his teachings worldwide.

Books by Paramahansa Yogananda

Available at bookstores
or online at www.yogananda-srf.org

Autobiography of a Yogi

Autobiography of a Yogi *(Audiobook, read by Ben Kingsley)*

God Talks With Arjuna: The Bhagavad Gita (A New
    Translation and Commentary)

The Second Coming of Christ: The Resurrection of
    the Christ Within You (A Revelatory Commentary
    on the Original Teachings of Jesus)

The Collected Talks and Essays
    Volume I: Man's Eternal Quest
    Volume II: The Divine Romance
    Volume III: Journey to Self-realization

Wine of the Mystic: The Rubaiyat of Omar
    Khayyam—A Spiritual Interpretation

The Yoga of Jesus

The Yoga of the Bhagavad Gita

The Science of Religion

Whispers from Eternity

Songs of the Soul

Sayings of Paramahansa Yogananda

Scientific Healing Affirmations

Where There Is Light: Insight and Inspiration for
    Meeting Life's Challenges
In the Sanctuary of the Soul: A Guide to Effective Prayer
Inner Peace: How to Be Calmly Active and Actively Calm
How You Can Talk With God
Metaphysical Meditations
The Law of Success
Cosmic Chants

A complete catalog of books and audio/video recordings — including rare archival recordings of Paramahansa Yogananda — is available on request or online at www.yogananda-srf.org.

Self-Realization Fellowship Lessons

The scientific techniques of meditation taught by Paramahansa Yogananda, including *Kriya Yoga* — as well as his guidance on all aspects of balanced spiritual living — are presented in the *Self-Realization Fellowship Lessons.* For further information, please ask for the free introductory booklet, *Undreamed-of Possibilities.*

SELF-REALIZATION FELLOWSHIP
3880 San Rafael Avenue • Los Angeles, CA 90065-3298
Tel (323) 225-2471 • Fax (323) 225-5088
www.yogananda-srf.org